Math Around Us

Backyard Math

Miguel Rosario

Cavendish
Square

New York

Published in 2015 by Cavendish Square Publishing, LLC
243 5th Avenue, Suite 136, New York, NY 10016

Copyright © 2015 by Cavendish Square Publishing, LLC

First Edition

Website: cavendishsq.com

This publication represents the opinions and views of the author based on his or her personal experience, knowledge, and research. The information in this book serves as a general guide only. The author and publisher have used their best efforts in preparing this book and disclaim liability rising directly or indirectly from the use and application of this book.

CPSIA Compliance Information: Batch #WW15CSQ

All websites were available and accurate when this book was sent to press.

Library of Congress Cataloging-in-Publication Data

Rosario, Miguel, author.
Backyard math / Miguel Rosario.
pages cm. — (Math around us)
Includes index.
ISBN 978-1-50260-141-4 (hardcover) ISBN 978-1-50260-146-9 (paperback) ISBN 978-1-50260-148-3 (ebook)
1. Arithmetic—Juvenile literature. 2. Counting—Juvenile literature. I. Title.

QA115.R68 2015
513—dc23

2014025533

Editor: Amy Hayes
Copy Editor: Cynthia Roby
Art Director: Jeffrey Talbot
Designer: Douglas Brooks
Senior Production Manager: Jennifer Ryder-Talbot
Production Editor: David McNamaraa
Photo Researcher: J8 Media

The photographs in this book are used permission and through the courtesy of: Cover photo by Hill Street Studios/Blend Images/Getty Images; Mark Herreid/Shutterstock.com, 5; akiyoko/iStock/Thinkstock.com, 7; Fuse/Thinkstock.com, 9; J8 Media, 11; natuska/Shutterstock.com, 13; Anthony Lee/Caiaimage/Getty Images, 15; JGI/Jamie Grill/Blend Images/Getty Images, 17; FreezeFrameStudio/iStock/Thinkstock.com, 19; © iStockphoto.com/aldomurillo, 21.

Printed in the United States of America

Contents

Today is a great day to play in the **backyard**.

How many swings do you see on the swing set?

There are **3** swings.

We are going to plant in the **garden**.

How many tools will we use?

We will use **3** tools.

7

Mom wears gloves to protect her hands.

How many gloves is she wearing?

Mom is wearing **2** gloves.

Worms help a garden stay healthy.

There are **3** worms. If **2** more joined them, how many worms would there be?

There would be **5** worms.

There are **6 flowers** on the plant.

If you picked **3** flowers, how many flowers would be left?

3 flowers would be left.

13

Ladybugs protect plants.

How many ladybugs do you see on the leaf?

7 ladybugs are on the leaf.

15

We are having a water balloon fight!

Maya is hit by **2** balloons.

Then she is hit by **3** more balloons.

How many balloons hit Maya all together?

5 water balloons hit Maya.

17

Now we grill hot dogs and **hamburgers**.

How many hot dogs are on the grill?

4 hot dogs are on the grill.

19

How many kids relax in the hammock?

3 kids relax in the hammock.

We had a great day in the backyard.

21

New Words

backyard (back-YARD) Green area at the back of the house.

flowers (FLOU-ers) The blossoms or bright parts of a plant.

garden (GAR-den) An area where plants are grown.

hamburgers (HAM-burg-gers) Patties of ground beef that are usually served on a bun.

ladybugs (LAY-dee-bugs) Small flying insects with red backs and dark spots.

Index

About the Author

Miguel Rosario lives in Ellicottville, New York. He has two beautiful daughters and a great big dog named Elmo.

About BOOKWORMS

Bookworms help independent readers gain reading confidence through high-frequency words, simple sentences, and strong picture/text support. Each book explores a concept that helps children relate what they read to the world they live in.